The 2007 Brown Center Report on American Education:

HOW WELL ARE AMERICAN STUDENTS LEARNING?

With sections on the nation's achievement, the mysteries of private school enrollment, and the impact of time on learning

December 2007
Volume II Number 2

by:
TOM LOVELESS
Director, Brown Center on
Education Policy

TABLE OF CONTENTS

Research assistance by:

KATHARYN FIELD-MATEER
Brown Center on Education Policy

THE 2007 BROWN CENTER REPORT ON AMERICAN EDUCATION

This is the seventh edition of the Brown Center Report on American Education. As in the past, the report consists of three sections. The first section examines the latest test score data on math and reading achievement. This year the analysis focuses primarily on results of the 2007 National Assessment of Educational Progress (NAEP), including a discussion of NAEP achievement levels.

The second section investigates a general theme or trend in education. This year the second section scrutinizes enrollment patterns in private and public schools. Section three looks at an issue of policy relevance. International test data are examined to see whether a relationship exists between national math scores and the amount of time students spend learning mathematics in different countries.

In past Brown Center Reports, no effort was made to tie the three sections together. The studies stood on their own. This year, however, the studies do have something in common: they investigate phenomena in education that—at least at first blush—do not make sense. Data on the percentage of students performing at "proficient" on the NAEP performance levels, for example, are routinely cited as evidence that U.S. schools are underperforming. But as a 2007 study by Gary Phillips of the American Institutes for Research shows, every nation in the world—including high flyers such as Singapore and Japan—would have significant numbers of students falling below proficient if they were administered the NAEP test. How can that be?

The second section's study of public and private school enrollment is precipitated by another oxymoron. Public opinion polls consistently show that the public considers private schools superior to public schools. Yet private school enrollment peaked around 1960 and has declined since then. People express a belief in public opinion surveys that they apparently contradict when selecting schools. What is going on?

The puzzle that is featured in the third section involves previous research on time and learning. When researchers have attempted to find a correlation between national test scores in mathematics and the amount of time different nations devote to teaching mathematics, no relationship has been found. Very odd. The correlation of homework and national test scores is stranger yet, with a negative relationship being the usual finding—the more homework given in math, the lower a nation's test score. We analyze these relationships using a different approach and come up with different findings.

Increasingly, education's most important questions are researched, debated, and decided with data. This is surely a healthy development as the field moves toward embracing the scientific methods that have benefited the intellectual disciplines that inform public policy. That said, with an election year now looming, it is important to be on the lookout for oversimplifications of either education's most pressing problems or its most promising solutions. Simply marshalling good statistics is not enough. The educational enterprise is exceedingly complex, and many cross-currents exist in educational data—evidence supporting one hypothesis, when looked at from another angle, might be seen as supporting an alternative. Even with sound data, many mysteries remain in American education. This issue of the Brown Center Report explores three of them.

Part I THE NATION'S ACHIEVEMENT

THIS PART OF THE BROWN CENTER REPORT CONSISTS OF TWO sections. First, the latest data from the National Assessment of Educational Progress (NAEP) are presented to evaluate how well American students are doing in reading and mathematics. The second section looks closely at a particular aspect of NAEP—the performance

levels used to describe different scores on the NAEP scale—and asks whether the "cutscores" for proficiency are set too high.

The 2007 NAEP test results showed small but statistically significant gains in both math and reading. Mathematics scores at fourth and eighth grade continued the steady progress registered since the main NAEP test was first administered in 1990. Both grade levels notched 2 point gains in scale scores. Table 1-1 reports the magnitude of the math gains in scale score points and years of learning. Figure 1-1 illustrates the upward trajectory of the scores. The gains indicate that fourth and eighth graders in 2007 knew more than two additional years of mathematics compared to fourth and eighth graders in 1990.

On the face of it, this is an amazing accomplishment. Previous Brown Center Reports have raised questions about such gains. The primary question concerns the content of the NAEP math tests. Students are clearly making progress, but at learning what kind of mathematics? Suffice it to say that students are making tremendous progress on

the mathematics that NAEP assesses, in particular, problem solving with whole numbers, elementary data analysis and statistics, basic geometry, and recognizing patterns. NAEP pays scant attention to computation skills, knowledge and use of fractions, decimals, and percents, or algebra beyond the rudimentary topics that are found in the first chapter of a good algebra text. In sum, we know that students are getting better at some aspects of math. But we do not know how American students are doing on other critical topics, including topics that mathematicians and others believe lay the foundation for the study of advanced mathematics. Thus, the years of learning gain must be taken with a grain of salt.

Reading scores also ticked up in 2007 (see Table 1-2 and Figure 1-2). Fourth graders have made good progress since scores bottomed in 2000, but eighth-grade scores have been flat since 1998. Both grades have added about 0.4 years of learning since 1992. In reading, the overall picture is of a glass half full and half empty. The half full

The years of learning gain (in math) must be taken with a grain of salt.

Math scores have been steadily increasing since 1990.

Table

1-1

	1990	1992	1996	2000	2003	2005	2007	1990–2007 Change	Change in Years of Learning
Grade 4	213	220	224	226	235	238	240	+27	2.2
Grade 8	263	268	270	273	278	279	281	+18	2.3

Years of learning based on 1990 score differences. Grade 4: 1 year equals 1/4th the difference between 4th and 8th grades (12.5 scale score points). Grade 8: 1 year equals 1/4th the difference between 8th and 12th grades (7.75 scale score points).

NOTE: Beginning with 1996, scores reported here include students who required special accommodations to take the NAEP

Source: NAEP data explorer, http://nces.ed.gov/nationsreportcard/nde/

part is that fourth-grade scores are now improving after falling during most of the 1990s. That is important. Fourth grade is a threshold year for learning how to read. Those who do not learn how to read by fourth grade face a struggle ahead, not only in reading but also in other subjects dependent upon reading, such as history. So the trend in fourth-grade scores is encouraging.

The discouraging part is that the gains that fourth graders have made are not carrying over to the eighth grade. The pattern for eighth graders is the opposite—gains in the 1990s and stagnant scores since 2000. This mirror image creates a troubling trend when the gains of cohorts are calculated. NAEP scores for fourth and eighth grades are calibrated on a common scale. Table 1-3 displays the score gains of three cohorts—the change in test scores between fourth graders for one particular year and the scores for eighth

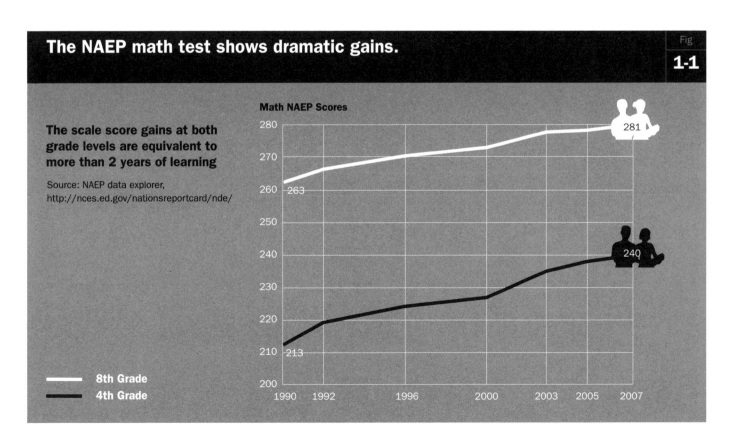

The NAEP math test shows dramatic gains.

Fig **1-1**

The scale score gains at both grade levels are equivalent to more than 2 years of learning

Source: NAEP data explorer, http://nces.ed.gov/nationsreportcard/nde/

Math NAEP Scores

8th Grade
4th Grade

graders four years later. Note that these are not real cohorts; the same children were not tested over a four-year interval. They are two representative samples of the nation's school children, however, so the approach is reasonable.

The fourth graders of 1994 gained 49 scale score points when they were next tested in eighth grade in 1998. The fourth graders of 1998 scored 49 points higher as eighth graders in 2002. The fourth graders of 2003 added 45 points when they were tested as eighth graders in 2007. The last cohort registered the smallest gain. The primary grades seem to be making headway in improving reading scores, but from fourth to eighth grade reading achievement is languishing if not deteriorating.

This trend cannot be good news for supporters of No Child Left Behind (NCLB). The fourth-grade NAEP measures what students have learned in school up to the

Reading scores ticked up between 2005 and 2007.

Table

1-2

	1992	1994	1998	2000	2002	2003	2005	2007	1992–2005 Change	Change in Years of Learning
Grade 4	217	214	215	213	219	218	219	221	+4	.4
Grade 8	260	260	263	—	264	263	262	263	+3	.4

Years of learning based on 1992 score differences. Grade 4: 1 year equals 1/4th the difference between 4th and 8th grades (10.75 scale score points). Grade 8: 1 year equals 1/4th the difference between 8th and 12th grades (8.0 scale score points).

NOTE: Beginning with 1998, scores reported here include students who required special accommodations to take the NAEP.

Source: NAEP data explorer, http://nces.ed.gov/nationsreportcard/nde/

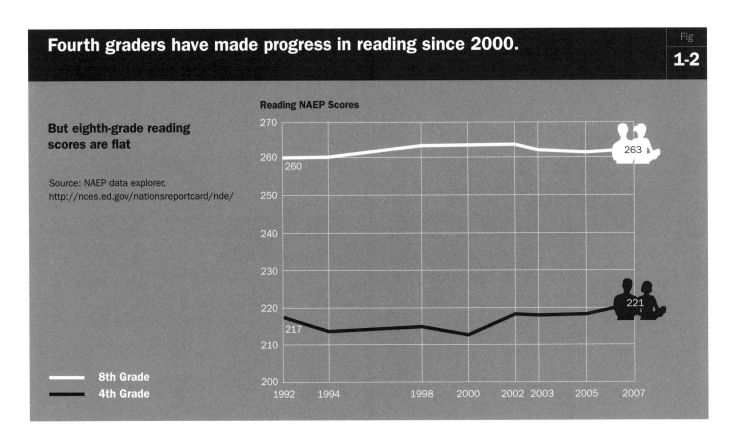

Fourth graders have made progress in reading since 2000.

Fig

1-2

But eighth-grade reading scores are flat

Source: NAEP data explorer, http://nces.ed.gov/nationsreportcard/nde/

Reading NAEP Scores

263

260

221

217

—— 8th Grade
—— 4th Grade

Progress in reading is deteriorating between 4th and 8th grades.

Table 1-3

Cohort	Score Gain
1994–1998	+49
1998–2002	+49
2003–2007	+45

Author's calculations from NAEP reading data.

Source: NAEP data explorer, http://nces.ed.gov/nationsreportcard/nde/

Introduction to NAEP

The National Assessment of Educational Progress (NAEP) is commonly referred to as the Nation's Report Card. Since 1969, it has been the only nationally representative and continuing assessment of what America's students know and can do in academic subject areas.

There are two NAEP test types: (1) the main NAEP gauges national and state achievement while also reflecting current practices in curriculum and assessment, and (2) the long-term trend NAEP allows reliable measurement of change in national achievement over time. These assessments use distinct data collection procedures and separate samples of students.

Since 1990, the math test on the main NAEP has been governed by a framework reflecting recommendations of the National Council of Teachers of Mathematics (NCTM). Beginning with the 2002 assessments, the number of students selected for an NAEP national sample for any particular grade and subject has been 150,000 or more.

From fourth to eighth grade reading achievement is languishing if not deteriorating.

beginning of fourth grade, the test being given in the fall of that year. Of the time students have attended school, only third grade is subject to the provisions of NCLB. Fourth through eighth grades, on the other hand, are fully within the purview of NCLB, and the 2003–2007 cohort, the one with the smallest gain in reading scores, was also the first to experience the law. With every little wiggle in test scores now attributed to NCLB—an endeavor that the law's supporters and detractors alike pursue with only superficial evidence—the disappointing eighth-grade reading scores loom as a political obstacle to NCLB's reauthorization. These data also cast doubt on anecdotal stories of a "Harry Potter effect," that after years of turning away from reading in favor of digital entertainment young people are returning to books for enjoyment. If they are doing so, it is not improving the NAEP scores of kids from about 10 to 14 years of age.[1]

Interestingly, the data do reflect the state of reading research. A solid body of research exists on beginning reading, factors influencing early reading difficulties, and

interventions that can help struggling young readers gain literacy skills. We know more about early reading acquisition and are attempting bolder policy initiatives in reading for primary-grade children. The report of the National Reading Panel highlighted this literature, and the Reading First program attempted to implement the findings in a national program.[2] Reading research focusing on fourth grade and beyond stands on shakier ground. Jeanne Chall, the legendary Harvard reading expert, began noticing in her work in the 1960s that reading test scores bogged down after fourth grade, a phenomenon she dubbed "the fourth-grade slump."[3] The fourth-grade slump is a riddle that has not been solved. The NAEP data testify to that. We need to learn much more about reading in the later elementary grades, middle school, and high school, including how to help students struggling with reading comprehension, if the gains in reading scores on the fourth-grade NAEP are to be extended and built upon in the later grades.

Is Proficiency on NAEP Set Too High?

This section examines NAEP performance levels. The No Child Left Behind Act identified proficiency in reading and mathematics as the goal for every student in the United States. The act left it to the states to define proficiency in both subjects—where, in other words, to set cutscores for proficiency on state tests. Many analysts have accused the states of dumbing down their tests or of making cutscores artificially low in order to inflate the number of students getting over the bar. The accusation rests on comparing the percentage of students that states say are meeting proficiency with the percentages reported by the NAEP. In almost all cases, states report many more proficient students than the NAEP.[4]

Studies in previous Brown Center Reports have shown that several assumptions buried within this story are wrong. The first assumption is that few students reach proficiency on NAEP because it is a rigorous test. Not really. None of the commentators who assert that NAEP is rigorous have conducted a content analysis to see what NAEP actually assesses. In mathematics, the eighth-grade NAEP test is dominated by problem solving with whole numbers, assessing mathematics that is usually taught by the end of third grade.[5] A significant number of eighth graders cannot solve two-step word problems involving whole numbers, that is true, but in the end, the only mathematics assessed by such items is whole-number arithmetic. Nothing can be construed about knowledge of more complex numbers (for example, fractions, decimals, percentages), knowledge that all eighth graders had better possess and yet is only minimally covered by NAEP. The recently released National Validity Study of NAEP verified that less than 15 percent of the eighth-grade NAEP math

test is devoted to fractions. Raw computation items, in which students add, subtract, multiply, or divide fractions or decimals— or even whole numbers for that matter— are virtually absent from NAEP.[6]

The second assumption is that states are "racing to the bottom" in response to NCLB. That assumption is not supported by the evidence. States reported larger percentages of proficient students than NAEP before NCLB, with no appreciable change in this practice since NCLB's enactment.[7] Moreover, the race to the bottom charge is confined to reading scores only. In math, states are reporting smaller gains since NCLB's enactment than the gains indicated by NAEP. And even if the states' data and definitions of proficiency are used to gauge progress, the goal of NCLB— that all students are proficient in reading and math by 2014—won't be met until at least 2069. No one is racing anywhere.

That brings us to a third assumption: that the NAEP performance levels—where the cutscores for performance levels have been set—are valid. Are students who score above the score for "proficient" truly proficient? Are students below this level truly falling short? Comparing NAEP scores with the results of international tests casts doubt on the validity of the NAEP cutscores. They appear too high. The analysis below focuses on math, but since the United States ranks higher in reading than math on international assessments, the standards for proficiency in reading are also certainly set too high. Most countries in the world would fail to meet the standard for proficiency if their students took the NAEP. Even large numbers of students in nations famous for academic excellence would fail to meet the requirement set by NCLB.

Before proceeding any further, some background information is necessary. NAEP has three achievement levels: basic,

Most countries in the world would fail to meet the standard for proficiency if their students took the NAEP.

Even high-achieving nations would not be "advanced" on NAEP
(basic = 469, proficient = 556, advanced = 637)

Table

1-4

Nation	Mean	Level of Nation's Mean
Singapore	605	Proficient
Korea, Rep. of	589	Proficient
Hong Kong, SAR	586	Proficient
Chinese Taipei	585	Proficient
Japan	570	Proficient
United States	504	Basic

Source: Revised version of table 11 from Gary W. Phillips, Linking NAEP Achievement Levels to TIMSS, Washington: American Institutes for Research.

No country meets the NAEP definition of advanced, which requires a TIMSS score of 637.

proficient, and advanced. Basic students have only learned the most elementary topics of a subject; proficient students have mastered what is expected at the grade level of the test; and advanced students demonstrate a breadth and depth of knowledge significantly beyond grade level expectations. Scores falling below the cutscore for basic are considered part of a fourth category: below basic. Describing these achievement levels in terms of student performance is a bit misleading in that NAEP does not produce scores for individual students. Nor for schools. In fact except for an occasional special study involving several large urban districts, NAEP does not produce scores below the state level. On the other hand, state tests report individual student scores. After schools show no improvement raising the number of students meeting proficiency for several years, the sanctions mandated by NCLB are implemented.

The Trends in International Mathematics and Science Survey test (TIMSS) also assesses eighth graders' knowledge of mathematics. Gary Phillips at the American Institutes for Research produced an eye-opening study that linked TIMSS and

NAEP. By equating math scores from the eighth-grade NAEP and eighth-grade TIMSS, Phillips was able to map the NAEP achievement levels onto the TIMSS scale. This allows for an estimate of how students in other countries would look in terms of the NAEP achievement levels. The comparison is not perfect. The two tests measure different content. Items involving fractions, for example, are nearly three times more frequent on the eighth-grade TIMSS compared to the eighth-grade NAEP. Although U.S. students' performance on both TIMSS and NAEP were used to link the two tests, students in other countries have not taken the NAEP. Whether they would in fact score at a particular level on NAEP is a projection, not an event that has been observed. Despite these shortcomings, the approach generates some reasonable estimates of how students in other countries would fare, whether they are basic, proficient, or advanced as defined by NAEP.[8]

Table 1-4 shows what several high-achieving countries' TIMSS scores look like in terms of NAEP achievement levels (subnational jurisdictions will be called "nations" or "countries" in this discussion for the sake of avoiding cumbersome language). No country meets the NAEP definition of advanced, which requires a TIMSS score of 637. Even Singapore, the highest-scoring nation in the world with a score of 605, falls 32 TIMSS points short of the advanced level. Five nations score at the proficient level—Singapore, Korea, Hong Kong, Chinese Taipei, and Japan. The United States' score of 504 is at the basic level, a little below the mid-point of this category, and 52 TIMSS points below the cutscore for proficient. Overall, 19 nations score below basic, 22 score basic, and 5 score proficient.

To put the U.S. ranking in perspective, if the growth made by eighth graders from 1990 to 2007—as noted above, an extraordinary gain of over two years of learning—continues at the same rate, the United States will join the group of proficient nations in 21 years and catch up with Singapore in about 41 years.[9] That assumes Singapore makes absolutely no progress of its own and its score stays the same. Such a gain would also represent more than four additional years of learning since 1990, on top of the 2.3-year gain that eighth graders have already accomplished. If you believe the NAEP scales and achievement levels, an eighth grader of 1990 needed to know about six more years of mathematics, equivalent to a 1990 sophomore in college, to be proficient at eighth-grade mathematics. And a test dominated by whole number problem solving—short on fractions and decimals, not to mention high school or college-level math—was crafted to determine whether the nation made progress toward this goal. That will not work.

The percentage of students in various countries scoring at "proficient" or above is displayed in Table 1-5. Only selected nations are shown to give the reader an idea of the wide span of performance. The same five Asian countries are at the top of the list, but even they would have significant numbers of students failing to meet proficiency. More than one quarter of Singaporean eighth graders are left behind in math by NCLB standards. Japan manages to get only 57 percent of students to proficiency. Some European nations perform dismally. England, Scotland, and Italy have more than 75 percent of students who are not proficient in eighth-grade mathematics. In Norway, 91 percent of children would score below proficient. That's a lot of Norwegian children left behind. African and Middle Eastern countries are grouped at the bottom of the list, and several of them have no children reaching proficiency (there is an error term which allows us not to take this literally).

The NCLB mandate is that schools will raise all children to a proficient level in reading and math by 2014. This requirement has changed the meaning of the term "proficient" from its original meaning as a NAEP achievement level. Media accounts often refer to proficient as "passing" and any score below that as "failing."[10] Even accountability experts have adopted such language. The Fordham Institute, for example, recently released a report that tells of a Michigan fourth grader whose "parents get word that she has passed Michigan's state test. She's 'proficient' in reading and math."[11] Whether the standard for "proficient" is realistic depends on what is meant by the term. It is the combination of the term's contemporary usage and high cutscores that make the NAEP "proficient" performance level highly questionable.

Discussion

All of this places NAEP in an Alice in Wonderland predicament in which nothing is really as it appears. In mathematics, we have a NAEP test with content that is too easy, with items posed in a manner that makes them difficult, and with cutscores for passing that are too high. A fictional scenario helps to illustrate the current situation. Imagine testing whether a child knows the alphabet—easy content. But instead of merely asking her to recite the alphabet, you ask that it be recited backward—posing an easy task in a way to make it difficult. Then, as a standard for proficiency, you require no pauses and a time limit of 10 seconds for this backward recitation—an unrealistic standard. Easy content, posed to appear difficult, with an unreasonable cutscore. And, most important, the only information that would be gleaned after putting a child through this exercise is whether she knows the alphabet.

Worldwide, NAEP proficiency standards leave a lot of children behind.	Table 1-5

Nation	Percent at or above Proficient
Singapore	73
Hong Kong, SAR	66
Korea, Rep. of	65
Chinese Taipei	61
Japan	57
Belgium (Flemish)	40
United States	26
Israel	24
England	22
Scotland	22
Italy	17
Norway	9
Morocco	1
Botswana	0
Saudi Arabia	0
Ghana	0
South Africa	0

Source: Revised version of table 10 from Gary W. Phillips, Linking NAEP Achievement Levels to TIMSS, Washington: American Institutes for Research.

Several prestigious organizations have reviewed the NAEP achievement levels and questioned their validity.

How did this happen? It all starts with content. The content of NAEP is governed by the NAEP framework. The original NAEP framework conceived of the main NAEP as a test assessing the ability to use math in context, in contrast to the long-term trend NAEP, which is a traditional, predominantly multiple choice test that has been in existence since the early 1970s. The long-term trend NAEP includes more raw computation items and fewer problem-solving items than the main NAEP. The problem-solving focus of the main NAEP affects the level of the mathematics on the test. In order to isolate the ability to solve problems and apply mathematics in context, item writers often lower the mathematical content of an item. Otherwise, the mathematics can get in the way of measuring the skills that the items are intended to measure. The 2004 Brown Center analysis of eighth-grade NAEP items coded "problem solving," for example, found a mean grade level of 3.4—middle of third grade—for the mathematics required to solve the problems.

Several prestigious organizations have reviewed the NAEP achievement levels and questioned their validity, including the Government Accountability Office, the National Academy of Sciences, and the National Academy of Education.[12] The National Academy of Education report concluded that the NAEP cutscores are too high and linked the flaw to the test's weak content: "The possibility that the cutscores are systematically too high is consistent with the finding from the panel's content-expert studies in reading and mathematics, which showed that because there were no advanced items to measure the content of the descriptions, the experts moved higher and higher on the score scale in search of such an item."[13]

The NAEP achievement levels must be reformed, especially with their increased

When it comes to gauging how well American students are learning, NAEP is the only game in town.

significance due to NCLB. Previous Brown Center Reports have recommended the reform of NAEP content in mathematics. The two are intertwined—the skills and knowledge that a test measures and a standard for what constitutes a "good enough" score. A good start would be to link the NAEP to other assessments, including international tests like TIMSS. If 25 to 50 percent of students in the top-scoring countries in the world fail to meet an American standard of proficiency, one wonders how realistic that standard is as a universal expectation. At the twelfth-grade level, the achievement levels should also be linked to AP exams. The scores of students who do extraordinarily well on AP calculus tests should correspond to an "advanced" achievement level on the twelfth-grade NAEP. By comparing NAEP levels to external benchmarks, the cutscores can be calibrated to better reflect student performance in math.

Analysts routinely refer to NAEP as "the gold standard" in American assessment. This tribute is largely based on the test's technical qualities and a number of innovations that NAEP pioneered in sampling and test construction. It is the only test of national achievement that surveys a random sample of students and administers tests in reading and mathematics across multiple grade levels. When it comes to gauging how well American students are learning, NAEP is the only game in town. The original purpose of the NAEP achievement levels was to report the national test results in a manner that the public could understand. Unfortunately, the NAEP achievement levels do just the opposite. It is time to get them right.

Part

II

MYSTERIES OF PRIVATE SCHOOL ENROLLMENT

M OST PEOPLE ASSUME THAT PRIVATE SCHOOLS ARE BETTER than public schools. More than half of the respondents to a 2004 Kappan Poll said they would send their children to a private school if vouchers were available covering the full tuition. This section of the Brown Center Report is about two trends in private school enrollment that do not make sense in light of the public's perception of

private school superiority. The first is that private schools' share of students peaked in 1959 and has subsequently declined. If private schools are so good and public schools so bad, why have private schools lost market share to public schools over the past few decades? And how could this happen at the same time that several well-crafted, well-publicized studies by eminent social scientists documented the virtues of private schooling? The second mystery has to do with the grade levels at which private schools lose students— in the transition to high school. Why are parents leaving private schools for public schools at precisely the time in a student's career when academic achievement means so much for college admission and later prospects in life?[14]

The Private School Advantage
In 1982, James Coleman published studies of private and public schools that rocked the foundation of the public school establishment.[15] One of the most prominent social scientists of his era, Coleman presented data from "High School and

Beyond," a massive national study of students who were tenth graders in 1980 and in twelfth grade two years later. The headline finding was simple: private schools are better than public schools. Students attending private high schools, in particular Catholic schools, gained about one grade level more on achievement tests than students attending public schools. Critics charged that Coleman had not taken into account the self-selection of private school students—that is, that kids in private schools may be better students initially or have parents more committed to education than the typical student. After all, parents go to a lot of trouble to send their kids to private schools, most notably, by paying private school tuition and supplying their own transportation despite having already paid taxes to fund public schooling. Coleman retorted that he had statistically controlled for selection bias so as to make a legitimate comparison.[16]

Later studies also praised private schools. Bryk, Lee, and Holland found that Catholic schools not only produce higher achievement scores, but they also serve "the common good" by boosting the education of poor and minority children. Building on Coleman's work, Bryk, Lee, and Holland estimated that minority students in Catholic high schools learn twice as much mathematics as their public school counterparts.[17] Derek Neal, a University of Chicago economist, found a Catholic school advantage in the graduation rates for both Hispanic and African-American students in urban areas, but no difference in the suburbs.[18] Catholic schools dominate the private school sector, comprising about half of total private school enrollment, so the positive findings about Catholic schools are crucial to comparisons of public and private schooling.

Coleman argued that private schools' effectiveness stemmed from the creation of social capital, the web of supportive relationships formed when like-minded parents choose a school with a mission they embrace. Bryk, Lee, and Holland lauded Catholic high schools for presenting a common academic curriculum and holding all students to a high standard. Neal and other economists saw the higher quality of private schools as the natural outcome of competitive markets. Instead of being assigned to schools based on residency, private school parents weigh all available options and choose the school that offers the best education.

These explanations rely on theories that depict parents as making rational choices when deciding where to send children to school. Favoring schools with a strong mission, seeking a rigorous curriculum that prepares students for college, rewarding quality when selecting from a market of schools—all of these phenomena hinge on what social scientists call "rational actors"—parents deciding to send their kids to private schools for clear, understandable reasons.

Such behavior makes private-public enrollment trends mysterious, since they do not look rational if private schools offer a superior education.

Enrollment Trends

Let's step back and examine some historical data. Table 2-1 shows the schools attended by 14- to 17-year-olds since the late nineteenth century. In 1890, most students left school by the end of eighth grade. Only 5.6 percent of 14- to 17-year-olds attended school. High schools had not caught on yet, and school attendance by 14- to 17-year-olds was rare in both the public and private sectors. At the dawn of the twentieth century, only about one in ten 14- to 17-year-olds attended school. Enrollment steadily picked up after 1910 and accelerated during the Great Depression, hitting 72.6 percent in 1940. The teenagers flocking into schools overwhelmingly attended public schools. The public school share of the 14–17 age group grew from 8.4 percent in 1900 to 68.1 percent in 1950, while private schools increased from 1.8 percent to 8.0 percent.

The private school share peaked at 9.3 percent in 1960. Since then, it eased to 7.7 percent in 2000 (and 8.0 percent in 2004, not shown in the table). The public school share of 14- to 17-year-old enrollment grew from 74.1 percent in 1960 to 83.5 percent in 2000. So this is interesting. At the same time distinguished scholars published study after study documenting the advantages of private over public schooling—with an emphasis on high school— parents were increasingly more likely to enroll their 14- to 17-year-old children in public schools, not private schools. The ratio of enrollments favoring public schools grew from about 8 to 1 in 1960 to more than 10 to 1 in 2004.

High school enrollment is indeed the culprit in the loss of market share. Table 2-2 disaggregates the enrollment data by grade level of school. Note that private school attendance in K–8 fell from 14.7 percent in 1960 to 12.5 percent in 2000, while at the same time, high school enrollment fell from 11.1 percent to 8.4 percent. Looking back, we can see that private high schools attracted a larger percentage of students than private elementary schools from 1890–1920. Private schooling was more popular

Trends do not look rational if private schools offer a superior education.

At the dawn of the twentieth century, only about one in ten 14- to 17-year-olds attended school.

School enrollment of 14–17 year olds, 1890–2000

(Percentage of students by sector and decade)

Table

2-1

Year	Overall	Public	Private
1890	5.6	3.8	1.8
1900	10.2	8.4	1.8
1910	14.3	12.7	1.6
1920	31.2	28.4	2.8
1930	50.7	47.1	3.7
1940	72.6	67.9	4.7
1950	76.1	68.1	8.0
1960	83.4	74.1	9.3
1970	92.2	83.8	8.4
1980	89.8	82.0	7.8
1990	92.5	84.1	8.3
2000	91.2	83.5	7.7

NOTE: Dates refer to spring semester, for example, 1890 is fall 1889.

NOTE: In fall 2004 8.0% and 86.9% went to private and public schools respectively.

Source: Author's calculations from Table 52 in the 2006 Digest of Education Statistics.

Elementary and secondary enrollment, 1890-2000

(Percentage of students by sector and decade)

Table

2-2

Year	Elementary		Secondary	
	Private	Public	Private	Public
1890	10.8	89.2	31.9	68.1
1900	7.6	92.4	17.6	82.4
1910	7.9	92.1	11.4	88.6
1920	7.1	92.9	8.9	91.1
1930	9.8	90.2	7.2	92.8
1940	10.3	89.7	6.5	93.5
1950	12.3	87.7	10.5	89.5
1960	14.7	85.3	11.1	88.9
1970	11.4	88.6	9.1	90.9
1980	11.7	88.3	8.7	91.3
1990	13.3	86.7	9.0	91.0
2000	12.5	87.5	8.4	91.6

NOTE: Dates refer to spring semester, for example, 1890 is fall 1889.

NOTE: For elementary students in fall 2004 12.3% and 87.7% went to private and public schools respectively. For secondary students the corresponding percentages were 8.4% and 91.6%.

Source: Author's calculations from Table 3 in the 2006 Digest of Education Statistics.

for older children than younger children. But not since then. Private high schools took an enormous hit from 1890 to 1940, recovered somewhat in the 1940s and 1950s, and then enrollment declined again in the 1960s. It has remained fairly stable since 1970. Private K–8 enrollment fell sharply in the 1890s, recovered slowly over the next half century, peaking in 1960, and then, like high schools, declined in the 1960s. Enrollment in private elementary schools has increased since 1970, from 11.4 percent to 12.5 percent in 2000.

The famous studies documenting a private school advantage relied almost exclusively on high school test scores, and yet high schools are where private sector enrollment declines the most. Enrollment patterns in recent years pinpoint that the drop off is occurring at the beginning of high school. We collected data on the number of students enrolled at each grade level in public and private schools. Table 2-3 compares the ability of the public and private sectors to hold students over three different grade spans: eighth to tenth grade, tenth to twelfth grade, and the entire period, eighth to twelfth grade. Data are presented for six different cohorts, students who were enrolled as eighth graders beginning in 1990 and then cohorts who were enrolled in eighth grade in every subsequent even-numbered year ending in 2000. For each cohort, the table reports public and private enrollment at the end of the interval as a percentage of enrollment at the beginning. If one million students were enrolled in private schools as eighth graders, for example, and two years later 800,000 were enrolled in private schools as tenth graders, an 80 percent figure would be entered for that cohort's grade 8–10 interval.

Let's follow the cohort of students who were eighth graders in 1990 (hereafter called "the 1990 cohort") as they progressed through school. Enrollment in private schools shrank significantly as the 1990 cohort entered high school. The number of tenth graders enrolled in private schools was only 86.7 percent of what it had been in eighth grade. At the same time, the number of students attending public schools grew. For the 1990 cohort, tenth grade enrollment in public schools was 102.2 percent of what it had been in eighth grade. In the transition to high school, students leave private schools and go to public schools.

From tenth to twelfth grades, the pattern is the opposite. Private schools keep more students—86.3 percent versus 83.1 percent for the 1990 cohort. Indeed for all six cohorts analyzed in the table, tenth-grade private school students are more likely than public school students to persist until twelfth grade. Public schools are more susceptible to students exiting after tenth grade. The private school students' greater persistence through the latter two years of high school seems to have widened in the 1990s.

Over the entire span of eighth to twelfth grades, public schools maintain a larger share of students than private schools. A consistent pattern is evident. Private schools lose students from middle to high school, and public schools gain students from the private school exodus. Once students make it to tenth grade, if they attend private schools they are more likely to stay in school until the senior year. After tenth grade, public school students are more likely to leave.

The net result is that—if we think of the private and public sectors as competing for students—public schools consistently win and hold a larger share of youngsters from eighth to twelfth grades. This may be changing. The public school edge shows signs of eroding in the 1990s. The gap favored public schools by 10.2 percent in 1990 (74.8 percent versus 85.0 percent) and shrank to only 4.9 percent in 2000 (82.2 percent versus 87.1 percent). The latest data for the cohort analysis ends with the 2000 base group, however, so whether the public school advantage has continued to slip will be borne out by later data.[19]

Cohort enrollment statistics, 8th–12th grades
(Percentage of students by sector)

Table 2-3

Cohort Base Year	8th–10th		10th–12th		8th–12th	
	Private	Public	Private	Public	Private	Public
1990	86.7	102.2	86.3	83.1	74.8	85.0
1992	82.2	101.0	90.0	81.5	74.0	82.4
1994	87.0	99.6	87.4	82.6	76.0	82.3
1996	85.2	100.6	91.6	82.4	78.1	82.9
1998	86.8	100.0	93.6	83.8	81.3	83.8
2000	90.2	100.9	91.1	86.4	82.2	87.1

Source: Public school enrollment: author's calculations from table 36 in the 2006 Digest of Education Statistics. Spring 1990 figure from table 42 in the 1995 Digest of Education Statistics. Private school enrollment: author's calculations from tables 10–13 of Private School Universe Survey years 1989–2004.

Discussion

Why are private schools losing high school students to public schools? Part of the answer is found in the difficulties faced by Catholic schools. As mentioned earlier they dominate the private school sector. In 1965, Catholic schools served 5.6 million students. In 2003, the number had dropped to 2.3 million. The decline occurred despite the nation's Catholic population approximately doubling since 1965. Yet now a summer does not pass without dozens of Catholic schools announcing that they will close their doors, especially in rust belt cities. According to Peter Meyer, the National Catholic Educational Association estimates that nearly 600 Catholic schools closed from 2000 to 2006. Twelve urban dioceses in the industrial cities of the East and Midwest lost almost 20 percent of their students.[20]

Several reasons are given for falling enrollments. Tuitions have soared to meet rising costs. Nuns once constituted the bulk of the teaching force in Catholic education, a source of cheap labor that has almost vanished. They were replaced by salaried teachers whose salaries must remain competitive with teachers' salaries in public schools. Old buildings in disrepair, families with financial resources moving from cities to suburbs, families requiring education services moving into urban

Private schools lose students from middle to high school, and public schools gain students from the private school exodus.

Catholic school enrollment suffered steep declines in the 1960s.

parishes—demographic changes have placed great strain on Catholic schools.[21]

Tuition also explains why high school is the point at which private schools lose students. In 2004, tuition at private secondary schools averaged $8,412, a significant leap from the $5,049 charged at the elementary level. Tuition at Catholic schools averaged $3,533 for elementary and $6,046 for secondary schools.[22] As children transition from elementary to secondary schools, families that cannot afford such hefty increases in tuition are forced to re-evaluate the relative advantages of private and public schooling. Although historical data on private school tuitions are spotty, Sol Stern reports that in 1965 the average annual tuition in New York City's Catholic high schools was $400. That compares with $6,000 today at Harlem's Rice High School, one of the city's lower-priced Catholic high schools.[23]

Other explanations point to cultural trends. Religious tolerance plays a part. The American Catholic schools were founded in the nineteenth century to provide schooling for families who felt that the larger society and its public schools were hostile to their interests, that the public schools would not provide the kind of education they desired for their children. This included religious instruction, to be sure, but also extended to a disciplined environment, structured curriculum, and high expectations. As mentioned above, Catholic school enrollment suffered steep declines in the 1960s. With blatant hostility toward Catholicism diminishing, Catholics more and more embraced secularized schooling. An article in the *National Catholic Reporter* quotes Michael Cieslak, director of research and planning for the Rockford, Illinois, diocese, as saying, "The whole issue of coming together, circling the wagons, that is no longer as important as it once was. For many people that was the raison d'etre for the whole Catholic school system and that simply isn't there anymore." To underscore the point, enrollments at evangelical Christian schools have surged in

the past few decades. Today, it is they who feel ostracized by mainstream institutions and who perceive a need to create their own schools.[24]

Factors other than religion also play a role. The fact that high school is the time when parents shift from preferring private to public schooling suggests something also may have changed related to child rearing. What has probably changed—and this point is admittedly speculative—are attitudes toward the schooling of teenagers. Parents offer their children more choices today and more say in schooling. Once children enter adolescence, they may prefer to go to school where kids in their own neighborhood go, not to a school across town. Moreover, parents want schools to offer more than academic learning. Social skills and "well-roundedness" are also very important. In a 1996 Gallup Poll, parents were asked to pick between the following: their oldest child being a straight-A student with only a few friends and extracurricular activities or a C student with a lot of friends and activities. By a two to one margin, they picked the busy, socially active C student. Perhaps all of the studies documenting higher test scores in private schools are identifying an attribute that parents find attractive but not decisive in selecting schools.[25]

The mysteries of the late-twentieth-century decline in private school enrollment are driven by a confluence of economic and social forces. Despite evidence that private high schools excel academically, overwhelmingly parents choose to send high-school-age children to public schools. Although that choice appears somewhat irrational, it could be that American parents do not consider academic quality the prime criterion for selecting schools, especially if the academic advantage incurs significant costs in tuition. This suggests it will take more than higher test scores to stem the decline of private schooling in the United States. It also suggests, in an era when school quality is the focus of much debate, that we have a lot to learn about what that elusive term really means.

Despite evidence that private high schools excel academically, overwhelmingly parents choose to send high-school-age children to public schools.

Part III

DOES MORE TIME MEAN MORE LEARNING?

I T IS ALWAYS COMFORTING WHEN SCIENCE VERIFIES COMMON sense. Several decades of formal experiments have concluded what is obvious to most people: time is essential to learning. Whether one is learning how to ride a bike, throw a baseball, solve algebraic equations, or unravel the causes of historical events, time is needed to acquire new

Countries where students spent a lot of time in math classes evidenced no consistent payoff in higher math scores.

knowledge and skills.[26] School reformers have embraced this truism by pushing to lengthen the amount of time children spend in school. Consider the academic calendar in the United States. In 1870, the school year ran 132 days. Supported by a century of compulsory attendance laws, schooling changed from a part-time activity of children to a dominant one. In 1870, the average student attended school only 78 days. That compares to 162 days in 1970.[27]

Calls for more time in school have not abated. In 1983, A Nation at Risk recommended an extra hour per day and up to 40 extra days per year in school.[28] In 1994, a national commission on school time reported to Congress, "We have been asking the impossible of our students—that they learn as much as their foreign peers while spending only half as much time in core academic subjects."[29] In 2005, the Center for American Progress, a left-leaning think tank, recommended extending both the school day and the school year as a matter of social equity. It noted that disadvantaged students

and English language learners have the most to lose when students are dismissed daily from school in mid-afternoon and given long summer vacations. An advocacy group, Strong American Schools, vows to make extending school time an issue in the 2008 presidential campaign and a National Center on Time and Learning was launched in the fall of 2007.[30]

Advocates of more time in school point to other nations as examples of what American kids should be doing. But a funny thing happens when analysts examine international test data and look for a correlation between time spent on education and academic achievement. They can't find one. Common sense seems to be wrong. Countries where students receive more math instruction score no higher on math tests than nations where students receive less instruction. The puzzle extends to time outside the classroom. Countries where more homework is assigned also evidence no advantage in achievement. In fact, they score lower than nations where homework is less prevalent. This pattern flies in the face of Julian Betts' research showing that homework significantly raises achievement. And yet the lack of a relationship between homework and national achievement is well known, having recently appeared in a popular anti-home-work book.[31]

Neither finding makes sense. Devoting more time to studying, whether at school or at home, does not appear to produce more learning. Of course, correlation does not prove causation. So it is possible that a differ-ent approach to the question would point in a completely different direction. This section of the Brown Center Report explores that possi-bility. Is it true that national achievement is unrelated to the amount of instruction that students receive? Is it also true that national achievement is negatively correlated with time spent on homework? Math is the subject on which the best data on these questions exist. We examine data from the math test of the Trends in Mathematics and Science Survey (TIMSS), an international assessment, to see if the findings of previous analyses still hold true. Our approach is different. Unlike previ-ous analyses, which looked for relationships in TIMSS data collected at one point in time, we model changes in instruction and home-work over several years and investigate whether those changes are related to changes in TIMSS scores.[32]

International Comparisons

David P. Baker, Gerald LeTendre, and several colleagues investigated the impact of time on achievement using data from the TIMSS of 1995. The TIMSS periodically assesses math and science achievement around the world and collects information on practices that may affect learning. Focusing on eighth-grade mathematics, the researchers found no relationship between national math scores and the amount of instructional time that

countries devote to mathematics. Countries where students spent a lot of time in math classes evidenced no consistent payoff in higher math scores. The researchers also discovered a negative relationship between math homework and achievement. Countries with heavier homework loads pro-duced lower TIMSS scores.[33]

These analyses were cross-sectional, examining the relationship of two phenome-na at a single point in time. A potential haz-ard to that approach, recognized by these careful researchers, is that cross-sectional correlations can mask the direction of a rela-tionship. Time in education is often allocated in a compensatory manner, making both instructional time and homework vulnerable to misinterpretation. An illustration of this can be found in an increasingly popular practice in the United States called "double blocking," in which schools schedule poor-performing students into two or even three periods of math in order to boost their learn-ing. Remedial students at these schools receive more instruction than high achievers. In a cross-sectional analysis, increased instructional time would appear correlated with low achievement.

The amount of homework assigned is also influenced by the level of the student receiving it. Homework may be assigned to low-performing students for the purpose of addressing skill deficiencies. In addition, students who take a lot of time to complete math homework may do so because they have troubles with the subject that slow them down. The situation becomes more complicated as students get older. Once stu-dents are tracked into courses based on prior achievement—a practice that begins in mathematics in middle school—high-ability students take more demanding courses that can require more homework. Students at either end of the distribution of mathematics

Pearson correlation coefficients for cross-sectional test scores and time variables
(eighth-grade TIMSS scores)

Table 3-1

	1995 Coefficient	2003 Coefficient
Instruction (I)	0.05	-0.20
Homework (H)	-0.22	-0.28
I+H	-0.18	-0.28

Source: 1995 and 2003 TIMSS reports and userguides.
See endnotes for a complete list of sources.

the sense that it compares each country to itself. By focusing on gains—regardless of the student making them—it obviates the problem of confounding time spent with the performance level of the student (or of the nation's students). The Baker and LeTendre work was conducted on 1995 TIMSS data. Since then the 2003 TIMSS data have been released, offering an opportunity to update their work by examining changes that occurred from 1995 to 2003.

Analysis

We computed the number of minutes of instruction that the average eighth grader in each country receives in mathematics during a school year. We did the same for homework. The calculations were based on data reported by teachers and principals. We then computed correlation coefficients to measure the relationship of national achievement in math to time spent on instruction and homework. TIMSS 1995 involved 45 nations. TIMSS 2003 involved 60 nations. Table 3-1 presents within-year correlation coefficients for 1995 and 2003, mirroring the approach of Baker and LeTendre. The correlation coefficients for math achievement and time spent on instruction (I) and homework (H) are shown. The I+H figure represents the annual time spent on instruction plus homework.

Correlation coefficients measure the relationship between two variables. Values range from +1.00 to -1.00, with a value of 0.00 indicating no linear relationship between the two variables, a value of 1.00 indicating a perfect positive relationship (as X increases, Y increases), and a value of -1.00 indicating a perfect negative relationship (as X increases, Y decreases). Variables with a correlation coefficient above zero are said to be positively correlated. Variable with coefficients below zero are said to be negatively correlated.

ability, then, may spend a lot of time on homework but for very different reasons. Cross-sectional analyses would mask these relationships.[34]

Students' performance levels can "cause" the amount of time devoted to instruction and homework just as easily as the reverse. Concluding that more instruction or more homework has no effect—or even a negative effect—on achievement would be misleading. Other technical pitfalls plague cross-sectional analyses of international data. Unobserved influences, such as cultural differences that may influence how homework or instruction are used, could lead to spurious conclusions about the effectiveness of spending more time on academic learning.

Looking at data collected at more than one point in time and seeing if the changes in two variables are correlated addresses some of these problems. Detecting potential causality is more likely—although not certain by any means. The approach "controls" for initial level of achievement and culture in

The correlation coefficients for our time variables and math achievement verify Baker and LeTendre's analysis. For both 1995 and 2003, neither instruction nor homework is related to math achievement at a statistically significant level. Instruction's relationship is neutral in 1995 (0.05) and mildly negative in 2003 (-0.20), and homework looks mildly negative both years (0-.22 and -0.28). The sum of the two activities is also mildly negative in both years, -0.18 in 1995 and -0.28 in 2003. The upshot is this: when examining cross-sectional TIMSS data from either 1995 or 2003, one cannot find evidence that the amount of time spent learning mathematics, either while receiving instruction or doing homework, is related to the amount of math that students actually know.

Exploiting the longitudinal nature of the data by examining changes from 1995 to 2003 leads to different findings. Note that a different question is now being posed. The question shifts from "In 1995 or 2003, did nations that spent more time on math instruction and homework also score higher on TIMSS?" to "Did nations that increased the time spent on homework and instruction from 1995 to 2003 also increase their TIMSS scores?" Twenty nations took the TIMSS test both years and collected the data on instruction and homework required to be included in the analysis.

Table 3-2 shows the correlation coefficients for change in time and change in test scores. Contrary to the cross-sectional analysis, the correlation for instruction is positive (0.42, p=.06). Homework appears neutral (-0.06). The combination of instruction and homework is mildly positive (0.27). Compared to the cross-sectional analyses, conclusions about all three time variables shift toward a more positive interpretation—from neutral to significantly positive for instruction.

Pearson correlation coefficients for changes in test scores and time variables.

Table
3-2

	Correlation coefficient
Instruction (I)	0.42*
Homework (H)	-0.06
I+H	0.27

*p<.10

NOTE: Time variables analyzed in units of minutes per year

Source: 1995 and 2003 TIMSS reports and userguides. See endnotes for a complete list of sources.

Instruction deserves additional scrutiny. The dot plot in Figure 3-1 clearly illustrates the positive association of instructional time and achievement. Notice the two outliers in the bottom part of the plot. The two dots represent Sweden and Norway. Outliers exert undue influence on correlation coefficients. Both nations experienced a large drop in math scores from 1995 to 2003—37 points for Norway and 41 points for Sweden. When these outliers are removed from the data, the instruction correlation coefficient for the remaining 18 nations is a very strong 0.62 (p<.01).

Lithuania, Korea, and Hong Kong all registered large gains in TIMSS scores while increasing the time spent on math instruction. But it can also be seen that the United States bucked the international trend, increasing its eighth-grade math score despite less time spent on instruction. The scorecard presented in Table 3-3 tells the story. Of the thirteen nations decreasing instructional time (those to the left of the

What is a Correlation Coefficient?

A Pearson correlation coefficient measures the strength of a linear relationship between two variables. The coefficient is always between -1.00 and +1.00. The closer a coefficient is to +/-1.00 the stronger a relationship is between two variables. 1.00 signifies a perfect positive relationship while -1.00 signifies a perfect negative relationship.

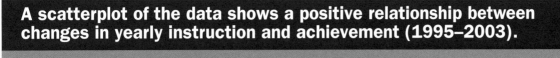

A scatterplot of the data shows a positive relationship between changes in yearly instruction and achievement (1995–2003).

Fig

3-1

Most countries that added instructional time increased their math scores.

Source: 1995 and 2003 TIMSS reports and userguides. See endnotes for a complete list of sources.

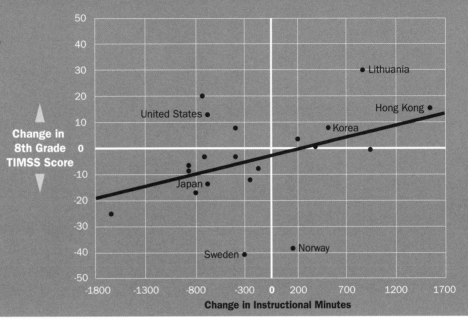

The apparent lack of a relationship between national measures of instructional time and achievement contradicts the findings of cognitive psychology as well as common sense.

vertical axis), ten posted lower scores in 2003 than they posted in 1995. Only three had higher scores. Of the seven countries adding instructional time (those to the right of the vertical axis), five experienced an increase in math achievement. Two countries experienced a decrease.

Discussion

Although statistically significant, the relationship of annual minutes of instruction with achievement should be put in real-world perspective. We ran a single factor regression model to gauge the magnitude of the relationship between instructional time and TIMSS scores. Every 100 minutes of added annual instruction is associated with a 1 point gain in TIMSS math score. Singapore, the highest scoring nation on

TIMSS, scores about 100 points higher than the United States. If one momentarily assumes that these findings are causal and predictive, the United States would gain about 4.5 points on TIMSS from adding an additional 450 minutes—about two weeks—of instruction in math. This would shrink the gap between the United States and Singapore by less than 5 percent. An extra 1,000 minutes of instruction would shrink the gap by about 10 percent.

Is the beneficial effect associated with adding minutes of instruction to each day or adding days to the year? Table 3-4 breaks down the TIMSS score gain that is associated with annual instructional time into two components: minutes per day and days per year. Do not forget that the analysis is only about math instruction. These estimates were produced from multivariate regression models that included both clock time (changing the amount of math instruction in a day) and calendar time (changing the number of days that math instruction is offered in a year). The average amount of math instruction for U.S. eighth graders was 45 minutes per day in 2003 (down from 49 minutes in 1995) over a total of 180 days (unchanged from 1995). The table reports the gain associated with adding 1,800 minutes of annual instruction by either increasing each day by 10 minutes or the year by 40 days.

Additions to both measures of time are positively related to achievement, but adding minutes each day appears more than twice as powerful. Adding 10 minutes per day to math instruction is associated with a 19.0 point gain in TIMSS score. Increasing the school year by 40 days is associated with a gain of 8.5 points. As a practical matter, extending the school day by 10 minutes has other positive attributes, in particular, being less disruptive to students, parents, and teachers. Small increases to the school day add up to a lot of time over an entire year. Lengthening the school year by 40 days would basically eliminate the summer break. Note that an increase of 10 minutes per day represents a 22 percent gain in instructional time. Remember that this extra time would have to be devoted exclusively to math instruction in order to reap the intended benefit in math test scores.[35]

As mentioned above, the apparent lack of a relationship between national measures of instructional time and achievement contradicts the findings of cognitive psychology as well as common sense. How have analysts explained the mystery? Most invoke a "leaky bucket" theory of educational time, in which the amount of instructional time designated by policy is diluted as it trickles down through the system. The time allotted to

Eighth-grade TIMSS scorecard

Table
3-3

	TIMSS score went up	TIMSS score went down
Increased instructional minutes	5 countries	2 countries
Decreased instructional minutes	3 countries	10 countries

Source: 1995 and 2003 TIMSS reports and userguides.
See endnotes for a complete list of sources.

instruction by policy is greater than the time implemented by teachers in the classroom, which in turn is greater than the amount of time students actually are engaged in learning. Unfortunately, the leaky bucket theory has rarely been tested empirically. In one notable case, studies by Rebecca Barr and Robert Dreeben of reading instruction in the 1980s uncovered considerable variation in the amount of allocated time teachers actually devoted to instruction. There is no reason to assume the same phenomenon cannot occur with math, at least in the elementary grades, in which typically one teacher teaches all subjects.[36]

Another common explanation is that instructional time is not used well, leading to recommendations of inservice training for teachers to boost efficiency. Simply doing more of the same in classrooms, this argument concludes, will not lead to more learning. The problem with this position is that there is not a lot of scientific evidence identifying effective instructional practices—and especially a paucity of evidence identifying effective practices that use time productively. Even less is known about effective, long-lasting professional development.

The effect of adding 1800 minutes of math instruction to the school year	Table 3-4

Increase in Instruction	Gain in TIMSS Score
10 minutes per day	19.0 points
40 days per year	8.5 points

NOTE: results of regression of change in TIMSS score on change in time variables.

Source: 1995 and 2003 TIMSS reports and userguides.
See endnotes for a complete list of sources.

Let's take stock of potential challenges to the analysis. What about confounding factors? Policymakers rarely reform just one aspect of schools. Changes such as additional time for instruction are usually implemented as part of a package of reforms—new textbooks, tougher qualifications for teachers, revised standards, accountability systems for schools and students. Nations have a lot of other things going on. This is a legitimate concern, especially if one of these unmeasured reforms is simultaneously related to increases in time and achievement. But such a wonderful reform would have to be adopted on a national level in several countries, have a noticeable effect on achievement, and somehow produce this beneficial impact across several national settings. Possible, but doubtful. It is far more reasonable to assume that the effect of 10 minutes added to instruction in Korea is similar to 10 minutes in France. Other reforms are not as fungible as time. Do not forget, too, that the countries that decreased instructional time and experienced depressed scores would be left out of such an explanation.

Is this sample of nations skewed? Only nations that participated in TIMSS in both 1995 and 2003 could be included in the analysis. Might that introduce unknown bias related to increases in instructional time? Maybe nations that emphasize achievement are also receptive to lengthening the amount of time spent in school and to participating in TIMSS in 1995 and 2003. No, these countries look similar to all the others participating in TIMSS, and they are quite diverse in terms of geography, national wealth, and levels of performance. Moreover, using changes in test scores as the outcome variable of interest should help control for the effects of a national inclination toward achievement. Even if the nations that produced gains on TIMSS are extraordinarily dedicated to

raising national test scores—or the ones that suffered score decline are extraordinarily indifferent to math achievement—it is doubtful that such a trait would change much between 1995 and 2003.

Again, a reminder that correlation is not causation. There is no way of telling whether the changes in instructional time led to the changes in national test scores in TIMSS from 1995 to 2003. The findings are presented to build upon previous work with TIMSS data that also analyzed correlations and found that math achievement is negatively associated with homework and neutral with respect to instructional time. Those findings were based on cross-sectional data. Analyzing changes in these variables over time produces a different set of findings. Both instructional time and homework appear more positive. The findings presented here—a neutral relationship of homework with achievement and a positive relationship for instructional time with achievement—bring the findings from international data more in line with the findings from other types of research on the impact of time on learning.

NOTES

1   Sonja Bolle, "*Harry Potter* and the Halo Effect" *The Los Angeles Times*, July 29, 2007.

2   National Institute of Child Health and Human Development, *Report of the National Reading Panel. Teaching Children to Read: An Evidence-based Assessment of the Scientific Research Literature on Reading and Its Implications for Reading Instruction* (Bethesda, Md.: National Institutes of Health, 2000).

3   Jeanne Chall, *Learning to Read: The Great Debate,* 1st ed. (New York: McGraw-Hill, 1967).

4   Analysts claim that states are engaged in a race to the bottom by dumbing down proficiency standards. Paul Peterson and Frederick Hess, "Johnny Can Read… in Some States. Assessing the Rigor of State Assessment Systems," *Education Next,* 5, no.3, Summer 2005. Paul Peterson and Frederick Hess, "Keeping an Eye on State Standards, A Race to the Bottom?," *Education Next,* 6, no. 3, (Summer 2006). Bruce Fuller and others, "Is the No Child Left Behind Act Working? The Reliability of How States Track Achievement," Working Paper 06-1 (Berkeley, Calif.: Policy Analysis for California Education, 2006).

5   Tom Loveless, *The 2004 Brown Center Report on American Education* (Washington: The Brookings Institution, 2004).

6   Phil Daro and others, *Validity Study of the NAEP Mathematics Assessment: Grades 4 and 8* (Washington: American Institutes for Research, September 2007).

7   Tom Loveless, *The 2006 Brown Center Report on American Education* (Washington: The Brookings Institution, 2006). Also see John Cronin and others, "The Proficiency Illusion," (Washington: Thomas B. Fordham Institute, October 2007).

8   Gary W. Phillips, "Linking NAEP Achievement Levels to TIMSS," (Washington: American Institutes for Research, April 2007).

9   The projected date at which the U.S. average NAEP score will reach proficiency was calculated as follows. From 1990 to 2007, eighth-grade math scores rose 18 points, a rate of 1.06 NAEP points per year. In the projection of TIMSS scores onto the NAEP scale, a gain of one NAEP scale score point between basic and proficient is equal to about 2.35 TIMSS scale score points. The 52-point gap on TIMSS between the U.S. and the cutscore for proficiency converts to 22.13 NAEP points (52/2.35), and the 101-point gap with Singapore converts to 42.98 NAEP points (101/2.35). The number of years to reach proficiency is 22.13/1.06 and to close the gap with Singapore 42.98/1.06, rounding both quotients up to the nearest whole number.

10   Liz Bowie, "Md., U.S. Testing Results Clash; Efforts to Evaluate Student Progress in Reading, Math Show Enormous Gap" *The Baltimore Sun,* December 25, 2005, pg. 1A. Ledyard King, "Tests Dumbed Down to Throw 'No Child Left Behind' Statistics" Gannett News Service, June 7, 2007.

11   John Cronin and others, "The Proficiency Illusion," (Washington: Thomas B. Fordham Institute, October 2007), p. 2.

12   Gerald Bracey, "A Test Everyone Will Fail" *The Washington Post,* May 3, 2007, p. A25.

13   Lori Shepard and others, *Setting Performance Standards for Student Achievement*, report prepared for the National Center for Education Statistics, (Washington: The National Academy of Education, July 1993).

14   In a 2004 Gallup Phi Delta Kappa Poll, 56 percent of the public said that with a full tuition voucher, they would pick a private school for their child to attend. Lowell C. Rose and Alec M. Gallup, Phi Delta Kappa International, "The 36th Annual Phi Delta Kappa/ Gallup Poll of the Public's Attitudes Toward the Public Schools," http://www.pdkmembers.org/e-GALLUP/kpoll_pdfs/pdkpoll36_ 2004.pdf (2004). For more public opinion data on private and public schools see William G. Howell, "Education Policy, Academic Research, and Public Opinion," Working Paper 2007–01 (Washington: American Enterprise Institute for Public Policy Research, May 2007), p. 15.

15   James Coleman, Thomas Hoffer, and Sally Kilgore, *High School Achievement* (New York: Basic Books, 1982). See also James Coleman and Thomas Hoffer, *Public and Private High Schools: The Impact of Communities* (New York: Basic Books, 1987).

16   Thomas Hoffer, Andrew Greeley, and James Coleman, "Achievement Growth in Public and Catholic Schools," *Sociology of Education* 58 (April 1985): 74–97. J. Douglas Willms, "Catholic School Effects on Academic Achievement: New Evidence from the High School and Beyond Follow-up Study," *Sociology of Education* 58 (April, 1985): 98–114.

17   Anthony Byrk, Valerie Lee, and Peter Holland, *Catholic Schools and the Common Good,* (Cambridge, Mass.: Harvard University Press, 1993).

18   Derek Neal, "The Effects of Catholic Secondary Schooling on Educational Achievement," *Journal of Labor Economics* 15, no. 1 (1997): 98–123.

19   Catholic schools continue closing in major cities. See Dennis Coday, "Catholic Schools Grapple with Forces of Change" *National Catholic Reporter,* March 25, 2005.

20   Peter Meyer, "Can Catholic Schools Be Saved?" *Education Next* 7, no. 2. (Spring 2007).

21   Sol Stern, "Save the Catholic Schools!" *City Journal,* (Spring 2007).

22   Thomas D. Snyder, Sally A. Dillow, Charlene M. Hoffman, *Digest of Education Statistics,* 2006 (Washington: National Center for Education Statistics, 2007), table 56.

23   Sol Stern, "Save the Catholic Schools!," *City Journal,* (Spring 2007).

24   Dennis Coday, "Catholic Schools Grapple with Forces of Change" *National Catholic Reporter,* March 25, 2005.

25   Stanley M. Elam, Lowell C. Rose, Rose, L. Alec M. Gallup, Phi Delta Kappan International, "The 28th Annual Phi Delta Kappa/ Gallup Poll of the Public's Attitudes Toward the Public Schools," http://www.pdkmembers.org/e-GALLUP/kpoll_pdfs/pdkpoll28_1996.pdf (1996).

26   Herbert J. Walberg, "Synthesis of Research on Time and Learning," *Education Leadership* 56, no. 6 (March 1988): 76-85.

27   Thomas Snyder, *120 Years of American Education: A Statistical Portrait* (Washington: National Center for Education Statistics, 1993), table 14. For the literature on time and learning, see B.W. Brown and D.H. Saks, "Measuring the Effects of Instructional Time on Student Learning: Evidence from the Beginning Teacher Evaluation Study," *American Journal of Education,* 94 no.2 (1986): 480–500.

28   The National Commission on Excellence in Education, *A Nation at Risk* (Department of Education, 1983).

29   National Education Commission on Time and Learning, *Prisoners of Time* (Department of Education, 1994).

30   Strong American Schools, "More Time and Support for Learning" (www.edin08.com/issues.aspx?id=76, [2007]). National Center on Time and Learning (http://www.timeandlearning.org/, [2007]).

31   Julian Betts finds that an extra half hour per night of homework in grades 7–11 produces two additional years of learning. Julian Betts, "The Role of Homework in Improving School Quality," Working Paper 96–16 (San Diego, Calif.: University of California, 1996). For anti-homework literature see Alfie Kohn, *The Homework Myth; Why Our Kids Get Too Much of a Bad Thing* (Cambridge, Mass.: Da Capo Press, 2006).

32   An exceptional example of this approach is Jan-Eric Gustafsson, "Understanding Causal Influences on Educational Achievement through Analysis of Differences over Time within Countries," in *Lessons Learned What International Assessments Tell Us about Math Achievement,* edited by Tom Loveless (The Brookings Institution Press, 2007), pp.37–64.

33   David Baker and Gerald LeTendre, *National Differences, Global Similarities: World Culture and the Future of Schooling* (Stanford, Calif.: Stanford University Press, 2005). David Baker, Gerald LeTendre, Motoko Akiba, and Alexander Wiseman, "Worldwide Shadow Education: Outside-School Learning, Institutional Quality of Schooling and Cross-national Mathematics Achievement," *The International Journal of Educational Policy, Research, and Practice,* 2, no. 1 (Spring 2001): 45–64.

34   Shirley Dang, "Schools Pile on English, Math Classes" *Contra Costa Times,* May 19, 2007.

35   We ran a multivariate model that also included a variable for national wealth. The results were about the same.

36   Rebecca Barr and Robert Dreeben, *How Schools Work* (Chicago: University of Chicago Press, 1983).

Notes for Part III figures and tables

For instruction see: Michael Martin and others, *School Contexts for Learning and Instruction, IEA's Third International Mathematics and Science Study* (Boston: TIMSS International Study Center, June 1999), Table 4.5 and Ina Mullis and others, *TIMSS 2003 International Mathematics Report, Findings from IEA's Trends in International Mathematics and Science Study at Fourth and Eighth Grades* (Boston: TIMSS & PIRLS International Study Center, 2004), Exhibit 7.3.

For homework see teacher background questions from 1995 and 2003 relating to frequency and duration of assignments. TIMSS 1995 Userguide, Population 2, Almanac bsalm52m1: isc.bc.edu/timss1995i/Database.html and TIMSS 2003 Userguide, bsalm5_3: timss.bc.edu/timss2003i/userguide.html.

For days in each country's school year see: TIMSS 1995 Userguide, Population 2, Almanac bsaml32m1: isc.bc.edu/timss1995i/Database.html and TIMSS 2003 Userguide, bsalm3_3: timss.bc.ed/timss2003i/userguide.html.

For cross-sectional achievement see: Michael Martin and others, *School Contexts for Learning and Instruction, IEA's Third International Mathematics and Science Study* (Boston: TIMSS International Study Center, June 1999), Table 1.5 and Ina Mullis and others, *TIMSS 2003 International Mathematics Report, Findings from IEA's Trends in International Mathematics and Science Study at Fourth and Eighth Grades* (Boston: TIMSS & PIRLS International Study Center, 2004), Exhibit 1.1.

For change in achievement between 1995 and 2003 see: Ina Mullis and others, *TIMSS 2003 International Mathematics Report, Findings from IEA's Trends in International Mathematics and Science Study at Fourth and Eighth Grades* (Boston: TIMSS & PIRLS International Study Center, 2004), Exhibit 1.3.